I0081523

Adult Coloring Stress Relief

with
Calming Paper Crafts

Leaves of Gold Press

Copyright © 2016 Leaves of Gold Press

All rights reserved. No part of this book may be reproduced or transmitted by any person or entity (including Google, Amazon or similar organisations) in any form or by any means, electronic or mechanical, including photocopying, recording or by any information storage and retrieval system, without prior permission in writing from the publisher.

National Library of Australia Cataloguing-in-Publication entry

Title: Adult coloring stress relief with calming paper crafts.

ISBN: 9781925110852 (paperback)

Series: Adult coloring stress relief ; 1.

Subjects: Color--Therapeutic use.

Paper work.

Coloring books.

Stress management.

Other Creators/Contributors:

Leaves of Gold Press, issuing body.

Dewey Number: 741.2

LEAVES of GOLD
PRESS

ABN 67 099 575 078
PO Box 9113, Brighton, 3186, Victoria, Australia
www.leavesofgoldpress.com

COLORING AND PAPER CRAFTS

Coloring in patterns and folding paper are enjoyable and absorbing activities that promote stress relief, mindful relaxation and creativity. They calm you down and help you to recharge.

Color the calming patterns and pictures inside this book and on the cover, then cut them out to make simple, useful gifts:

- 7 cardboard bookmarks
- 4 patterned paper boxes with lids
- 16 classic bookplates

This adult coloring book provides beautiful, soothing designs to ease you into a state of relaxation.

Join the natural stress relief trend sweeping the globe!

ADULT COLORING STRESS RELIEF

Book 1: Adult Coloring Stress Relief
with Calming Paper Crafts

Book 2: Adult Coloring Stress Relief
with Calming Card Games: Spades

Book 3: Adult Coloring Stress Relief
with Calming Card Games: Hearts

Book 4: Adult Coloring Stress Relief
with Calming Card Games: Diamonds

Book 5: Adult Coloring Stress Relief
with Calming Card Games: Clubs

BOOKMARKS

THE back and front covers of this book have been designed so that after you finish coloring the patterns you don't have to put the book on a shelf and forget about it — instead you can create useful and decorative bookmarks.

The history of bookmarks is as old as the history of books. Bookmarks can be made of card, fabric, paper, metals like silver and brass, silk, wood, or cord. Some lie between the pages, while others are designed to clip on. They can be plain rectangles or fancy shapes.

With pencils or felt-tipped pens, simply color the patterns on both sides (or on one side only if you prefer), then cut them out.

We have left a small space between the bookmarks to make them easier to trim. If they were touching and you missed the line by a fraction, one bookmark would end up being too thin and the other too wide.

Bookmarks make lightweight hand-made gifts, easy to post to family and friends overseas.

Fleur de cerisier - 1898
Alfons Mucha

BOOKPLATES

A bookplate, sometimes called an 'ex-libris', is a small, decorative label pasted into a book, usually on the inside front cover, to indicate its owner. 'Ex-libris' is from the Latin ex, 'from' and libris, 'library', meaning 'from the library of'. Historically, bookplates began in the Middle Ages as simple inscriptions.

Bookplates typically bear an image, motto, coat-of-arms or other motif. Popular images include the 'library interior—a term which explains itself—and 'book-piles'.

The name of the owner usually follows an inscription such as
- from the books of...
- from the library of...
- ex libris....

Collecting and exchanging bookplates became a craze during the 19th century. In 1891 a group of dedicated collectors founded the Ex Libris Society in Britain.

Bookplates can indicate the provenance of old books, ensure the return of books you have lent to others, or adorn your books with beautiful pictures you have colored yourself!

How to make your own bookplates

Simply color in these genuine vintage designs (or leave them black and white if you prefer), cut them out and paste them inside the front cover of your favourite books. Write your name and/or other contact details in the spaces provided. The bookplates are printed only on one side of each page so that you can apply glue to the blank side. Wrinkle-free glue sticks work best.

We have left a small space between the bookplates to make them easier to trim. If they were touching and you missed the line by a fraction, one bookplate would end up being too thin and the other too wide.

Rediscover the joy and stress relief of creativity!

EX·LIBRIS·

EX LIBRIS

THIS BOOK

PAPER BOXES

Paper boxes are lightweight, decorative containers that can be easily made out of paper sheets. Use them to hold small, light items such as gifts, paper clips, candies, hair clips, beads etc.

Color the relaxing patterns in this book, then use scissors to snip out the colored paper pages and make your lidded box.
Alternatively, make the base of the box from plain white paper and the lid from your patterned paper.

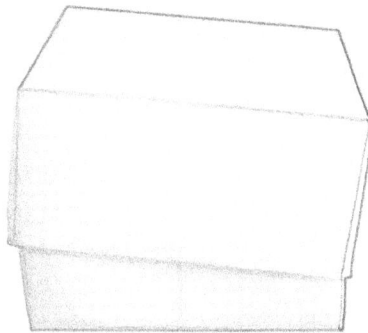

How to make your own paper boxes

Simple method (Kirigami)
This method is really simple, because you make four small, straight cuts in the paper to make the folding easier.
Kirigami is a variation of origami that includes cutting of the paper (from Japanese 'kiru' = to cut, 'kami' = paper), rather than just folding the paper as is the case with origami.
The instructions are on page 14.

Classic method (Origami)
This origami method uses no cutting. Find out how to do it on page 18. In Japan, an origami paper box is sometimes called a 'masu box'.

Rediscover the joy and relaxation of creativity!

SQUARING YOUR PAPER

Start with two paper squares, one for the lid and one for the base. The base must be smaller than the lid, so that it will fit.

To make sure each paper is exactly square, fold one corner of the paper until it meets the opposite edge, forming a triangle. Make sure the edges meet exactly.

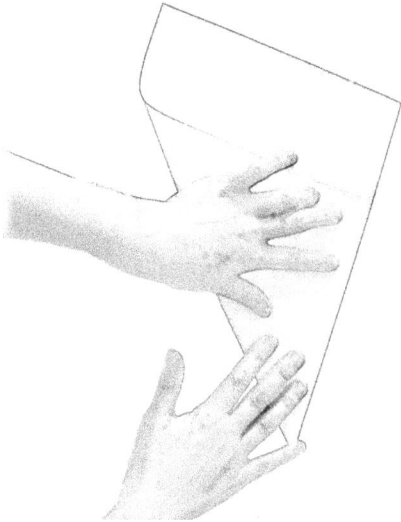

Cut the piece for the lid into a square.

Draw a line 9mm (3/8") from the edge on the second piece and cut along the line to make a slightly smaller square

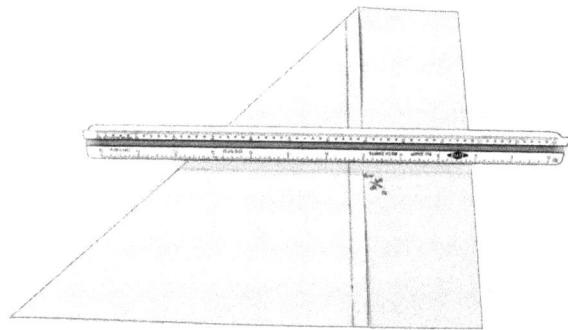

Discard the cut-off strips or save them for other projects.
Now you have two paper squares; a slightly larger one for the lid and a smaller one for the base.

PAPER BOX: SIMPLE METHOD (KIRIGAMI)

- After coloring in the design, cut two pieces of paper out of the book and make sure they are square. One should be bigger than the other. (see page 13).
- Fold one square along the diagonal and open it out again. This creates a nice sharp crease as a guide. Do the same along the other diagonal.

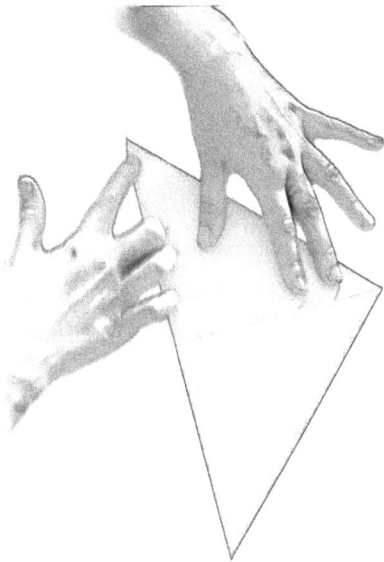

- Fold all 4 corners of the paper into the center.

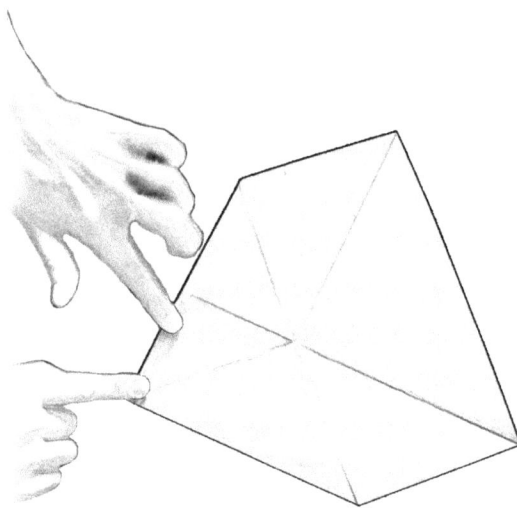

- Fold one side of the square into the center, as shown, then do the same to the other side.

- Open the square and fold back the corners, one by one. The tips of the corners should meet the edges as precisely as possible.

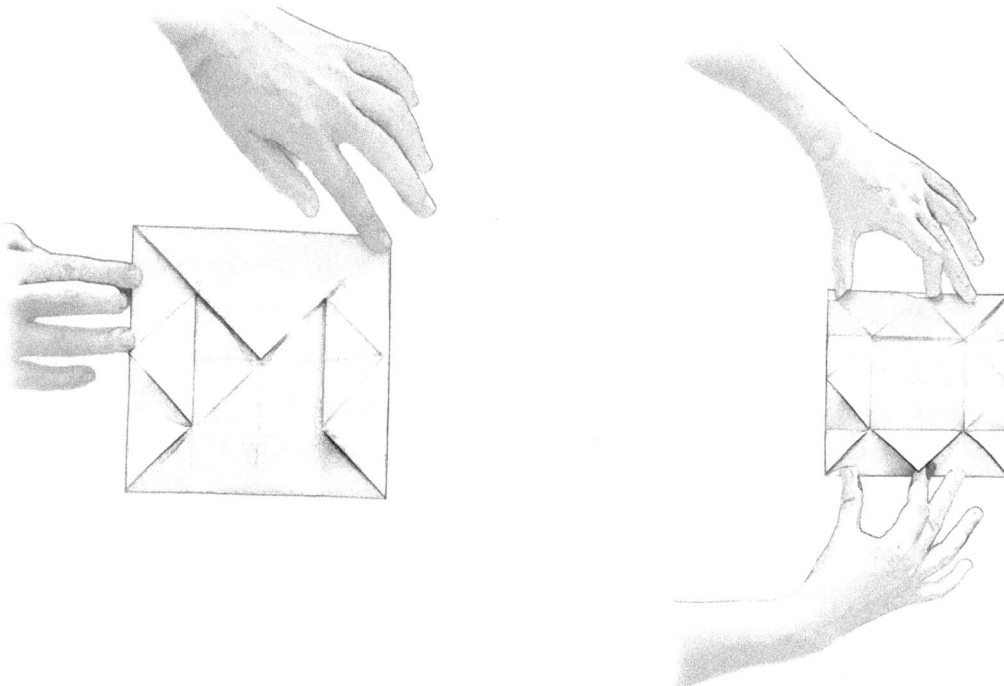

- Make 4 cuts into the right and left sides of the folded paper. Be careful not to cut too long or too short. Cuts should be just long enough so that the two flaps — one on the right and the other on the left — can open.

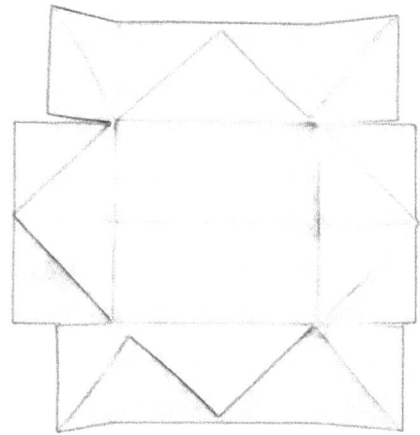

- Pull out the right and left flaps.

- Now fold in the two sides. The lid begins to take shape.

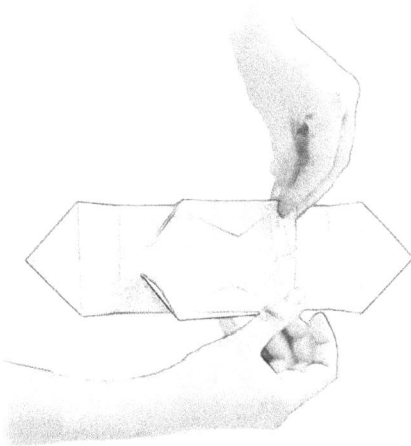

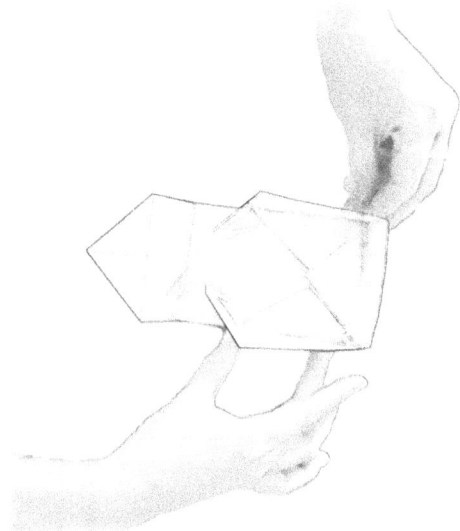

- Fold the flap over the side and down. Do the same with the other flap and the lid is finished.

- To make the base of the box, use the smaller paper square and simply follow the instructions for the lid.

- Fit the lid onto your beautiful paper box.

- When your lidded box is finished, if the flaps in the bottom won't stay down, use a little glue. Glue sticks are recommended.

PAPER BOX: CLASSIC METHOD (ORIGAMI)

- After coloring the design, cut two pieces of paper out of the book. Make sure they are square, and one is bigger than the other (see page 13).

- Follow the instructions for the simple Kirigami box above, but stop before you make the scissor cuts.

- Instead of cutting the paper, unfold the flap on the right and the flap on the left.

- On one side, tuck in the corners while folding the larger flap over and into the bottom of the box. This is the tricky part but do not be discouraged!

- Do the same thing on the other side.

- Repeat all these steps on the other piece of paper to make the second part of the box.

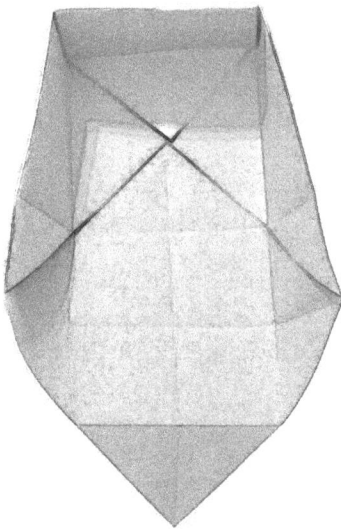

Fit the lid to the base and enjoy using your pretty paper box.

PIMPERNEL BULRUSH

THE pattern on the other side of this page, with its profusion of lively flowers and foliage is typical of William Morris's art. This design, created in 1896, adorned the walls of the dining room at Morris's home, Kelmscott House, in Hammersmith, UK.

GOLDEN LILY

ON the reverse of this page is a Morris & Co. wallpaper design called 'Golden Lily'.

A beautiful pattern of entwining lily stems and tendrils, it was designed in 1899 by William Morris's apprentice, John Henry Dearle.

Morris & Co. prints had a resurgence of popularity in the 1970s. At its peak the wallpaper fabric "Golden Lily" was selling 5,000 metres a month.

BOWER

ON the reverse of this page is William Morris's pattern 'Bower'. Morris created this wallpaper design in England in 1877. The wallpaper was manufactured in London by Jeffrey & Co, using color woodblock prints on paper.

"Although for [Morris] repose is an essential quality which the designer should pursue, this does nor mean that designs should be blank and staric; rather that they should give up something of the relaxed pleasure of a garden. A wallpaper should be able to turn a room into a bower, a refuge, without insisting on its presence in the room with us."
~ Ray Watkinson

TULIP AND WILLOW

ON the reverse of this page is William Morris's furnishing fabric pattern 'Tulip and Willow'. Completed in 1873, it is the second textile he designed. In 1883 it was manufactured by block-printing on cotton textile in in his own factory at Merton Abbey, Wimbledon, using the ancient and painstaking indigo-discharge method he admired above all forms of printing. It is a slow and expensive method. Discharging removes the color from fabrics and is the opposite of dyeing. Morris preferred using natural dyes and avoided synthetic coal-tar dyes, which he said produced 'hideous colours, crude, livid and cheap'.

Textiles printed with the 'Tulip and Willow' pattern were used for curtains, wall-coverings and furniture upholstery. The original colours were indigo and golden-yellow.

STRAWBERRY THIEF

The pattern on the reverse of this page is called 'Strawberry Thief'. It is one of William Morris's most popular repeating designs for textiles. Morris was inspired by the thrushes that stole fruit from the kitchen garden of his countryside home, Kelmscott Manor, in Oxfordshire, England.

'To print the pattern Morris used the indigo-discharge method. This was the first time anyone had successfully used this method to print a pattern on textiles which incorporated red (natural alizarin dye) and yellow (natural weld dye) in addition to the blue and white background.

'Strawberry Thief proved to be one of Morris's most commercially successful patterns. This printed cotton furnishing textile was intended to be used for curtains or draped around walls (a form of interior decoration advocated by William Morris), or for loose covers on furniture.'

Wikipedia: Strawberry Thief (William Morris).
Retrieved 18 February 2016

MORRIS SEAWEED

ON the reverse of this page is a pattern called 'Morris Seaweed'. It was one of the most popular designs created by William Morris's protégé John Henry Dearle, who designed it in 1901. The serpentine pattern captures the swaying and twining of water-plants buffeted by underwater currents and is clearly influenced by the Art Nouveau movement.

Originally printed in yellow ink and the natural blue plant dye 'woad', 'Seaweed' was intended for use as wallpaper.

GOUDY INITIALS

IN the early 1900s Frederic W. Goudy designed the floriated initials which are printed on the reverse of this page. For several decades Goudy was the Art Director for Tolbert Lanston, the American inventor of the first mechanical typesetting system.

Under Goudy's direction Lanston cut the matrices for casting lead type and released them as 'Goudy Initials, No 296'. The fine craftsmanship of this typeface has been loved by typographers for many years.

The font Goudy Initials is listed as 'free for commercial use'.

Enjoy coloring these beautiful letters.

M N O
P Q R
S T U
V W X

NOTES ABOUT BOOKPLATES

SOME of the mottoes on the vintage bookplates in this book may seem strange. '*Spiro spero*', for example; this is from the Latin phrase '*dum spiro, spero*', meaning 'while I live, I hope' or 'while there's life, there's hope.'

> "Yet ah! That spring should vanish with the rose!
> That youth's sweet-scented manuscript should close
> The nightingale that in the branches sang,
> Ah, whence and whither flown again who knows?"

Inscribed on one of our bookplates, the above verse is from the Rubáiyát of Omar Khayyám, translated in the 19th century by Edward FitzGerald.

"No book is worth anything that is not worth much" is another motto on one of our bookmarks. It is an abstruse quote from Ruskin, while '*sibi et amici*' translates as 'he and his friends.' referring to a man whose friends are his books.

The phrase "*vulnus opemque fero*" is Latin for 'I carry a wound (or a weapon) and a remedy.' This motto refers to a medieval Saxon superstition that the horn of the unicorn was not only an effective weapon but also had healing properties.

'*Labor, Content Ailleurs, Theoria*' These words are written on a bookplate designed in 1870 for Oscar Browning. 'Content ailleurs' is French for 'happy elsewhere'. Theoria is Greek for 'contemplation', while 'labor' means work or toil.

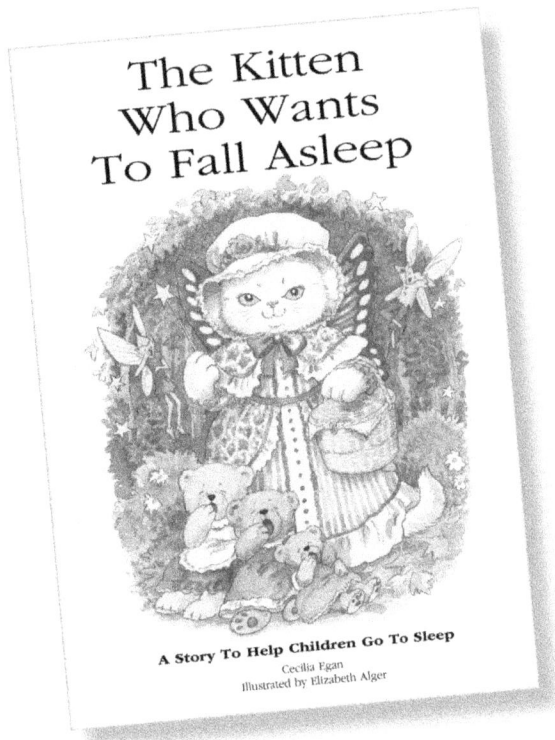

THE KITTEN WHO WANTS TO FALL ASLEEP
A Story to Help Children go to Sleep

Amazon rank #1 New Release in the category 'Sleep Disorders'

Children sometimes find it hard to get to sleep.

What if you could read them a bedtime story incorporating powerful psychological methods to help them fall asleep quickly, easily and without drugs?

IS FOOD MAKING YOU SICK?
The Strictly Low Histamine Diet

People can suffer from histamine intolerance without being aware of it.

The symptoms are many and widely varied. They can affect the digestive system, the respiratory system, the skin and other parts of the body. These problems may endure throughout our entire lives if we continue to consume large amounts of histamine.

The good news is, if we can understand what is happening and why, we can treat or prevent this widely unrecognized condition.

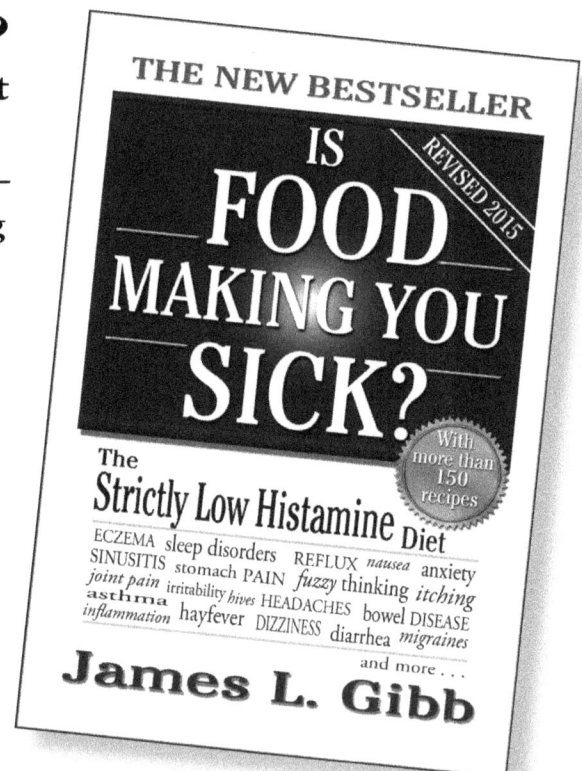

ADULT COLORING STRESS RELIEF
WITH CALMING CARD GAMES

Adult Coloring
Stress Relief
with
Calming Card Games
DIAMONDS

Adult Coloring
Stress Relief
with
Calming Card Games
SPADES

Adult Coloring
Stress Relief
with
Calming Card Games
CLUBS

Adult Coloring
Stress Relief
with
Calming Card Games
HEARTS

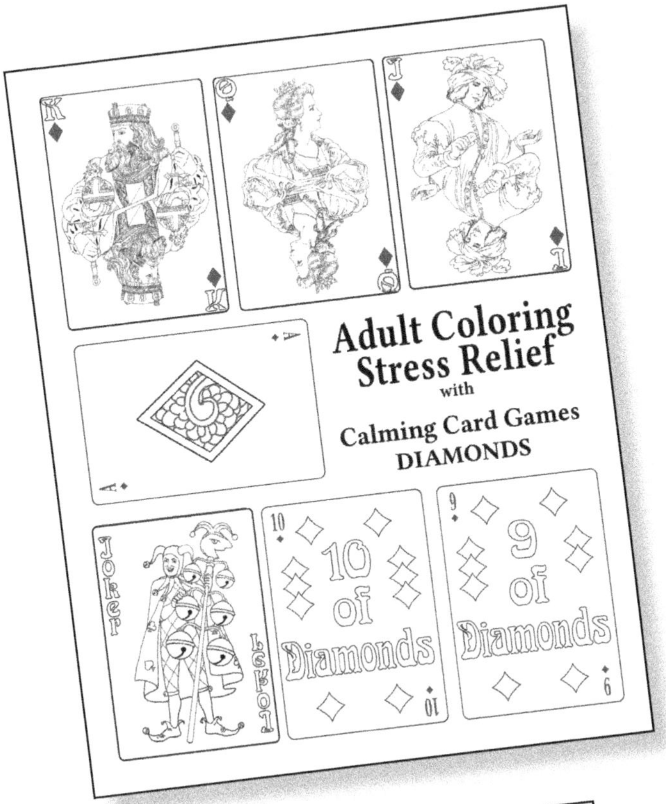

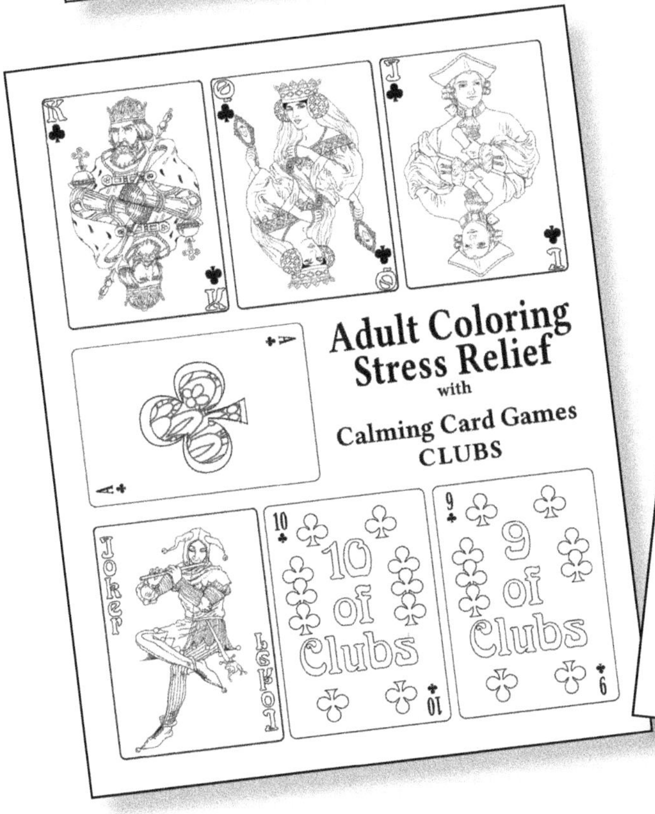

www.ingramcontent.com/pod-product-compliance
Lightning Source LLC
Chambersburg PA
CBHW061410090426

42740CB00026B/3495